The Oscillations Within

Taranandini Rath

Made with ❤ on the BookLeaf Publishing Platform
www.bookleafpub.in
www.bookleafpub.com

Dedication

To *the Supreme Soul, The Almighty*,
The eternal source of
light, wisdom, and guidance,
My compass on life's voyage.

To the earthly replicas of The Divine,
My beloved parents, Bou and Papa,
The nurturing sources of
love, care, and strength,
My anchors in the oscillations of life.

This book is a tribute to the divine spark that
dwells within us all.

Acknowledgments

"Look at the sky, we are not alone. The whole universe is friendly to us and conspires only to give the best to those who dream and work."
— *Dr. A.P.J. Abdul Kalam*

The journey of creating *The Oscillations Within* has been a profound and transformative experience—an exploration of life's contrasts, its quiet moments, and its storms. This book exists because of the unwavering support, guidance, and inspiration of the remarkable people and experiences that have shaped my life.

Never in my wildest dreams did I imagine writing a book, though I have always been inclined toward poetry since my student days. As I transitioned into the digital realm and navigated various stages of life, my love for writing quietly receded into the background. However, during the COVID-19 pandemic, at the inauguration ceremony of *my father, Sri Radhamadhab Rath*'s debut children's novel—a great teacher and an inspiration in his own right—my passion for poetry was rekindled.

Surrounded by *my revered parents, Papa and Bou,* along with *my caring Kakei, eminent teachers, authors, and poets,* I was profoundly moved by their inspiring words and presence. This transformative moment was made even more special by the unwavering encouragement of *my dear husband, Akshaya; my loving sister and brother-in-law, Tareni* and *Satyabrath;* and *my cherished friend, Rutuparna,* who stood lovingly by my side.

My heartiest gratitude to *Dr. Sudipta Mishra,* a renowned author and dear friend, who opened doors for me by introducing me to vibrant literary communities. Through these, I connected with prolific poets *Jai Prakash Albert* and *Mariya Ashley,* whose guidance and encouragement have been instrumental in my growth as a poetess.

One fateful day, *BookLeaf Publishing's* program appeared on my Facebook feed, and it felt like destiny calling. Their platform nurtured the budding poetess within me, and with the unwavering support of *Hemapriya, Roosha,* and *Arushi,* I found the courage to bring this dream to life.

To *the superb team at BookLeaf Publishing,* thank you for believing in my vision and providing invaluable support throughout this journey. Your dedication and professionalism have given me the platform to share my voice with the world.

The transition from software engineering to writing has been far from solitary. I am deeply grateful to *my esteemed parents-in-law, Bapa and Maa, as well as all the respected elders of my wonderful family.* My heartfelt thanks extend to *my inspiring circle of friends, well-wishers, mentors, and colleagues at the workplace,* whose unwavering support and encouragement have been invaluable throughout this journey. Each person I've encountered has left a lasting imprint on this work, infusing it with the warmth and generosity of countless hearts.

To *my inquisitive, knowledge-seeking nieces* and *nephews* from the family; *my loving littlest niece, Shivanshi; and with all heart, my adored son, Adhrit*—your laughter, curiosity, and boundless energy remind me daily of the beauty in life's simplest moments. You are my greatest inspiration, and this collection would not be the same without the joy and love you bring into my life.

To *my illustrious teachers,* thank you for shaping my thoughts and nurturing my curiosity. Your wisdom has been indispensable to my growth, both as a person and as a writer.

To *every life* I have encountered—thank you for being part of my journey. Each interaction has left an indelible mark on my heart, teaching me lessons, sparking my curiosity, and deepening my understanding of the world. To *every still moment* that offered me clarity, solace, and inspiration—I owe my words to your quiet power.

To *Mother Nature,* thank you for being my eternal muse. Your beauty, serenity, and profound wisdom have enriched my soul and inspired many of the verses in this collection.

Above all, my heartfelt gratitude goes to *the Supreme Soul* for being my guiding light and source of strength. Your Divine presence has anchored me in turbulent times and inspired my creativity.

Finally, to *every reader* who picks up this book—thank you for joining me on this journey. May you discover a piece of yourself within these pages, feeling inspired as you resonate with the rhythm of the verses.

With heartfelt gratitude,

Taranandini Rath

Preface

Life is an intricate dance of highs and lows, a rhythmic oscillation between joy and sorrow, hope and despair, chaos and calm. In this ever-shifting balance, we often find ourselves suspended between the pull of what was and the tug of what could be. It is within these moments of flux that our truest selves emerge—raw, vulnerable, and beautifully human.

The Oscillations Within is my attempt to capture this eternal dance of emotions. Each poem is a thread woven from the tapestry of experiences, feelings, and observations that have shaped my life. From moments of quiet introspection at twilight dawn by the sea to the profound stillness of dusk by the lakeside, this collection traverses the spectrum of human emotions. It celebrates the resilience of the human spirit and the profound beauty found in embracing life's uncertainties.

This book is not just a collection of verses but a reflection of the journeys we all undertake. It is for the dreamers who chase their aspirations despite the odds, for the seekers who find solace in nature's embrace, and for the wanderers who navigate the ebb and flow of life with courage and grace.

May you find echoes of your own story within these words as you turn these pages, for we are all connected by the shared rhythm of existence! May this collection inspire you to embrace the oscillations within your own life, to find peace in the chaos, and to revel in the beauty of being human!

With heartfelt gratitude,

Taranandini Rath

Contents

1. Oh Almighty!

Oh Almighty!
You must be proud
Of originating Homo sapiens,
Your most fascinating creation, through evolution.

You must think
He is so beautiful, so winsome,
But alas!
Don't You know what reality is?
Oh Omniscient!
Glance at him—
He is so ugly, so gruesome.

If You are right,
Then why?
Why is the air thick with brutality?
Why are there bloody shows?
Why the massacre, for power, for money?
Why is there fear,
Everywhere, every moment?
Fear of disguised devils,
Fear of his own replica?

May Your ethereal guidance
Enlighten his dusty mind,
Fill his malignant heart
With peace and harmony...!

May there be a tsunami
Of Your celestial blessings,
Washing away...
All the woes and agonies,
Leaving behind only tranquility.
May that peace metamorphose
This poignant world into paradise...!!!

2. The Solace

Wandering in that heaving road,
Yet solitary I am...!
Which is the way... where should I go?
Obtain no answer, I scream though.
With illuminated lights that city glitters
Why with utter darkness, my heart roars?
With the twilight hues, the galaxy smiles
Why into the black hole my world mingles?
Laden with gloom, I go astray in the crowd
Plethoric nostalgia pinches my pensive mood.

Searched you only in
that oblivious city,
I am lost in the
poignant globe;
None feels pity.

All are lively...
Yet I am still...
Hold my hand;
Show me the path,
Is my earnest will...!

I hunt for your tender care
Every nook and corner;
The search goes in veins;
My heart starts to murmur.
Had I wings, I would fly away;
Land up in my abode,
Where your endless warmth
Is always overflowing!

The Moon rises in my eyes...
In the blue sky, the stars twinkle;
Drenched in the silvery drizzle,
The panorama starts to sparkle.
How peacefully white clouds float
In the azure sky!
The serene vista slowly takes
All my blues away...
Sitting beside the lake;

I can feel you in this heavenly world;
In whirls of joy,
My doleful heart gets unfurled.
Almighty cannot be everywhere,
So made you...!
Departed by a thousand miles;
So solaced by the splendid view...!!!

3. The Monarch

Standing on the heap of carcasses,
His deafening voice screamed—
"Dare to defeat me?"
Far, wide deserted war field,
Scorching sun,
Blazing noon,
Pale dying trees,
Scattered corpses,
Feasting vultures,
Fresh flesh and drying blood
Celebrated his victory...!
Yes! He was emperor the great
Of sobbing hearts...!
Years passed by...
He died... people rejoiced with sheer glee—
"Oh finally... The demon returned to hell...!"

Sitting beside the ailing beds
In her tiny sickbay...
Her healing tone softly asked—
"Are you feeling better now?"
Smiling and content eyes,
Cold crystal moon,
Tranquil night,
Cool breeze,
Jovial trees,
Dancing doves,
Aromatic air,
Celebrated her divine aura...!

Yes! She was a pauper, but a princess
Of sanguine hearts...!
Years passed by...
Her soul departed...
People lamented with utter grief—
"Alas! Our angel returned to heaven...!"

In annals of history, we come across the two,
No need to say, the real monarch is who...!!!

4. The Illusion

You said, "I am free..."
I built castles in the air...!
My tiny heart danced with a whirl of joy.
Spreading my little wings,
I got ready to own that vast azure sky.
I sang my happiest song
That echoed in that distant hill,
I dared to touch the silvery moon
Amid my utmost thrill...!

Soon after my dreamy yet gleeful voyage,
I came across disguised devils everywhere.
Oh alas! How gruesome were they
To my utter nightmare...!
The burning breeze woke me up...
In a narrow cage, I found me
With torn feathers and tied wings.
How can a choked throat sing
But only screams...!

That far distant hill laughed at me
And I could only see a giant sun
And its blazing beams...!

Caged by the so-called civilized world,
Every pulse of my pensive heart cries aloud...!
Standing in the graveyard of my dreams,
"You are free...!"
I still hear from the crowd...!!!

5. Gratitude

When whirls of thoughts
Create ripples in my mind,
Flocks of memories and magma of emotions
Get intertwined...!
Trillions of neurons and axons wire together,
Impulsively those solemn moments transpire after.

Like thousands of piercing arrows,
Your dismaying words penetrate
My friable pericardium.
With a ruptured heart... I ventured out
For the sublime equilibrium...!

While I seek for the sanguine sunshine
Your mocking words eclipse my pensive mind...!
Entangled with hundreds of confines,
Who are you to jeopardize
My cherished dreams?
Why should I owe explanations to you,
When I am the Michelangelo
Of my life's foundations...?

Oh... how beautifully
You pretend with phony succor!
I crumble... I perish... and you cheer.

You dissuade me with evil desire...
Like that nebula,
I collapse to find the North Star,
That glorifies my path
And navigates my life's canoe
And my whole universe spins
With a rejoining hue...!
Don't dare to consider me
That fragile little bird...
Which can be caged
With your abundant limitations...!
Winning the mosaic of battles...
As a Phoenix... I rise from the ashes
Of my shattered ambitions...!

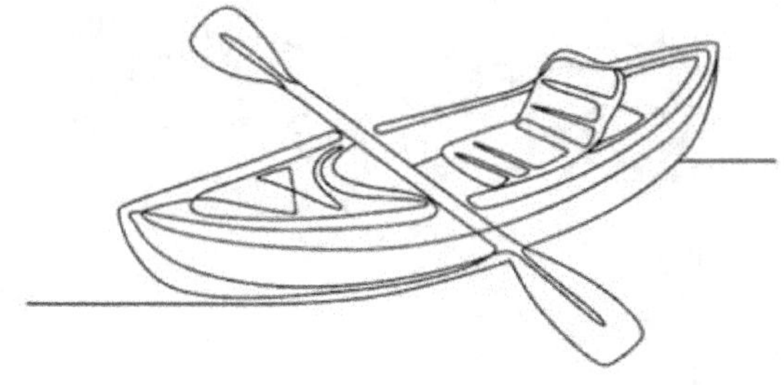

Treasuring all your dejections
As the propelling force
Amid the crest of waves
My life's canoe sails through...
With sincere gratitude, let me convey

"A heartfelt Thank You...!"

6. My Sunlit Desire

Sometimes,
My forlorn heart bleeds tears,
Reminiscing about
the inaugural glimpse of yours...!
Oh, alas!
Entwined with hundreds of wires and tubes,
You were deep asleep
in that tiny plastic cradle...!

Like blaring thunders,
Those constant beeps and alarms
Cracked my cochlea apart
With their deafening din...!
While my succumbed heart
Longed for sanguine revival...
They started to dispirit your frail body,
And blame me for your premature arrival...!

I oscillated between qualm and lassitude,
With the tsunami of desolation...
I was submerged in utmost solitude...!
Wrecked by whips of penetrating words,
I held your fragile fingers
with a shivering hand...!

You smiled with a bright arch
and whispered to me...
"Oh, Mother...!
They are blind... they cannot see...
I am the Almighty's benevolent miracle...
I emerge,
I reach the pinnacle of waves
In the ocean of roseate oracles...!
They are feeble,
How much I am empowered...
They cannot measure...!
I am strong... I am abundant...
Omnipotent blessings I treasure...!
These little odds of life...
I am enough to overpower...
Wipe your tears... let's chase the dreams...
Together, the world, we shall conquer...!"

With celestial elation, I started to utter...
"Oh, Son...!
You are the seraphim angel I am blessed with,
You, the eternal sunshine of my life,
Expelling all the gloomy sheaths...!
I just desire to be
The splendid nurturer, you deserve...
With lyrical symphony, my brittle heart
Resonates with the orchestra of verve...!!!"

7. The Graffiti on My Heart

Away from the hustle and bustle
Of my monotonous life,
With sheer thrills, once I ventured
Into the lush green valleys.

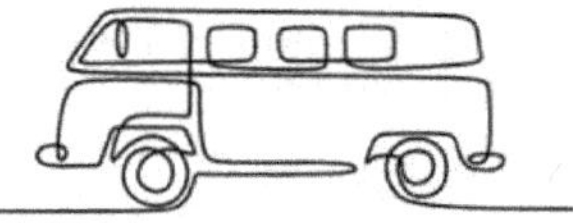

The harmonious chirping birds
Hummed the welcome song,
With whirls of joy,
I got submerged...
In the ocean of golden daffodils...!
Suddenly a delightful drizzle
Magnified my euphoria,
I could smell petrichor...
Like the florets of the dancing dandelions,
My buoyant heart started to flutter...!

While listening to the rhythm
Of the falling rain,
I was in the hunt for shelter
In that solitary lane.
A granny and her grandchild,
Sailing paper boats,
An amiable sight I stumbled across,
Near a blurry windowpane.

"Would you like to join us?"
The old lady invited jovially.
"How gracefully
You retain your childhood...!"
I exclaimed gleefully.

With a bright arc
The elated lady smiled
"Oh, young lady...!
We are never too old
To make our inner child celebrate.
With every zeptosecond,
Our cells may grow old,
Yet, our beautiful spirit should remain
palpitated...!

Let's embrace those wrinkles
And the silver-tinted hair
They bear eloquent testimony...
To the time,
In the colossal cosmos, we share...!
Just to live and enjoy is not
What we are here for
Be kind and caring to everyone
For happiness galore!
Let's offer gratitude for every little joy,
We are blessed with...
A grateful heart is always a magnet
For a plethora of miracles!

Growing old is the eternal law
Of the galactic universe
With gentle gestures...
In the path of compassion...
Let's traverse...!

Filling palettes with colors
Of peace and harmony
Let's paint our life canvas
And create a magical journey...!
Before bidding adieu to
The dreamy voyage called life,
Wrap up the expedition within...
Discover your real self
And make the world
A better place to live in...!"

Enthralled by her fathom of wisdom...
I stood spellbound,
Traveled just to quench my wanderlust soul...
Got startled to be on cloud nine
With the knowledge, profound...!

Gosh! Peeping through the fluffy clouds,
The sublime sunbeams shined
Bridging across the azure horizon...
A radiating rainbow
Captivated my pensive mind...!!!

8. A Letter to My Little One

Dear Son,

Way before I met you,
The day I listened to
The cardiac rhythm of your tiny heart
I have fallen in love with you...!

Oh...! An elfin life started growing inside me
My life canvas is filled
With palettes of radiant hues...!
The first moments of you, are always treasured,
Wrapped with Almighty's kindest blessings...
In my solemn life, you are the conductor
Of the orchestra of verve...!
Your angelic face stole away all my agonies
All the piercing pain evaporated
With just a glimpse of you...
In the ocean of euphoria,
My buoyant heart merrily sails through...!

Oh, my beloved...!
You are what my world spins around
Amazed by your purest love,
I stand spellbound...!
Oh, my baby...!
With every passing moment,
Your innocent giggles... tiny laughs...
Brighten my day!

You load my auricles and ventricles
With immense affection in a profound way...!
Like the rainbow of hope,
You have appeared in my life's gray sky...
With every warm embrace and tender kiss,
You spread a spectrum of joy!

We took birth together...
You as my son and I as your mother...
Like that hummingbird,
Humming the symphony of life...
I am flying in a reverse order...!
You never judge me...
Your sparkling eyes always twinkle with love,
Swaddled with abundant sunshine,
In your heart, I found my little cove...!

Holding your little hands,
While I try to teach you,
How to lead a life with full content...
Dispersing the little joys,
How to live life is what you gave me the intent...!
Every day I am falling in love with life...
Falling in love with you more
With your hearty smiles and new curiosities,
I find happiness galore!

Oh, my little one...!
I am always there for you.
Sometimes...
Like that North Star, shining bright,
Sometimes...
Like that cold crystal Moon in the night,
I am there to navigate your life's canoe...
Sometimes
Like that shimmering Sun on the far horizon,
I am there in your path
To make you glisten like the morning dew...!

Oh, dear...!
You are going to complete...
Seven years of roller coaster ride
In our beautiful world...!
With growing years,
Like the sublime petals of an animate flower,
The good and the bad days get unfurled...!
On good days,
Let you be humble and offer gratitude...!
Let bad days shape you...
And may you conquer
All the battles of life in great magnitude...!!!

With heaps of love and light,
Your Mother

9. The Sublime Harbor

Leaving the safe quay
To chase the buoyant waves,
The lone seafarer set out
On his maiden expedition.

With the cool breeze and the placid sea,
Like florets of the sunlit dandelion,
His exploring soul fluttered...
And spreading the golden rays,
The crimson sun went
For rest on the far horizon...!
Oh, how splendidly
The pearly stars canopied the sky!
Oscillating with the twirling waves
The ferry glided through
The spectrum of joy...!

Suddenly, the dark clouds
Veiled the crystal moon,
Alas! The gleeful voyage
Metamorphosed into a nightmare soon...!
Rippling the surface of the sea,
The winnowing wind created giant waves,
Oh gosh!
A brewing storm roared
With pelting rain and bellowing thunders,
The electric lightning bolts scared
The mariner with spine-chilling quavers...!

Bobbing like a cork in the swollen-up sea,
The tiny yacht keeled and tilted
Witnessing the emblazoned
Sky and rain lacerating
Gripping the tiller,
The desolate man stood shivering!

Standing firm like a rock,
His life insights flashed in the blink of an eye!
A calm heart is the biggest anchor,
Be the storms in life or the sea
Life may throw a thousand reasons to quit,
But to the heart, let faith adhere.
Believe in prayers,
Miracles do happen to those
Who conquer their fears.
Sailing through the crest of gigantic waves
Throughout that fateful night,
He hunted incessantly for a distant shore.

The silvery beams suddenly dazzled;
A shadow whispered
"A calm sea never does,
The storms shape a skillful sailor
Don't be afraid; just sail your canoe...,
Patience and perseverance
Will get you the desired harbor...!"
Stunned by the enlightened words,
The sailor turned around
With a serene presence he got enthralled,
But none was found.

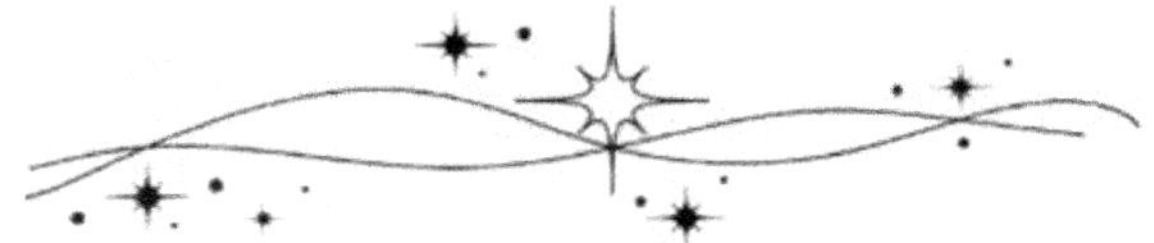

Wild waves calmed down as the hours passed,
The blue sky was adorned with twilight hues;
The darkest night ended
The capillary waves gently propelled the jib
And happily, the yacht sailed.
As a harbinger of harmony,
The orange sun emerged,
Turning the azure horizon tranquil
Fighting all the odds,
Finally, the sailor discovered
The sublime harbor with utmost thrill...!!!

10. My Ethereal Expedition

Amidst the quiet ripples,
My life's canoe begins to sail
Laden with buoyant memories,
In the thoughts of the stream, nostalgia prevails.

Beyond the realm of the chaotic world,
Beneath the azure sky,
I embrace solitude
With the quest for the soul
I voyage for an inward journey,
A symphony of waves broadens my latitude!

With a palette of radiant hues,
Painting the canvas of purple sky,
On the far horizon,
The golden sun begins to descend
Welcoming the tranquil twilight
Paddling my canoe,
I reach the shore as my thoughts transcend!

By the crackling campfire,
Silhouettes of thoughts
Whisper in the silent breeze.

Galvanized by flickering flames,
My quills embark on a serene flight,
Pouring my wavering thoughts
Onto pristine paper
I find the seraphic joy
In silver moonlight!
Healing the labyrinth of piercing pains
Ink flows like a sacred stream,
Washing all my agonies away,
As soulful prayers,
The earnest scribbles
Connect me to the cosmic divine...!

11. A Tale of Triumph

As the flickering flame
Of the candle shakes
With the gust of wind,
Your spirit may tremble,
You may feel alone,
Deprived of a friend...!

As they laugh at your defeat,
Ridicule without end.
But this is your journey, dear,
Follow your dreams, not the herd.
Embrace your rareness, carve your path,
Defying each mocking word.

Hemlock of wounding words,
May blaze your heart,
Ignite your spirit, tear you apart.
They say you fall into another category,
Since you don't merge with the flocks.
Oh yes, prove them right!
Different minds shape the world,
Breaking the numerous locks.
Those with different lenses can truly see,
While billions come and go,
Mingling into dust, endlessly.

Like the ugly duckling,
Misplaced in the throng,
Mocked for being different,
For seeming "wrong."
You may be in a brood where you don't belong,
A beautiful cygnet, with strength to hold on.
Endure the trials, let the doubts be gone,
For soon you'll rise, a radiant swan.

Like Maleficent's curse,
Life may hurl many tribulations,
A plethora of piercing words,
Like the prick of a sharp spindle,
May try to silence your spirit,
Slipping you into endless sleep.
But with burning desire,
You will break every evil spell,
Metamorphosing failures into ashes,
The fire within conquers every hell!

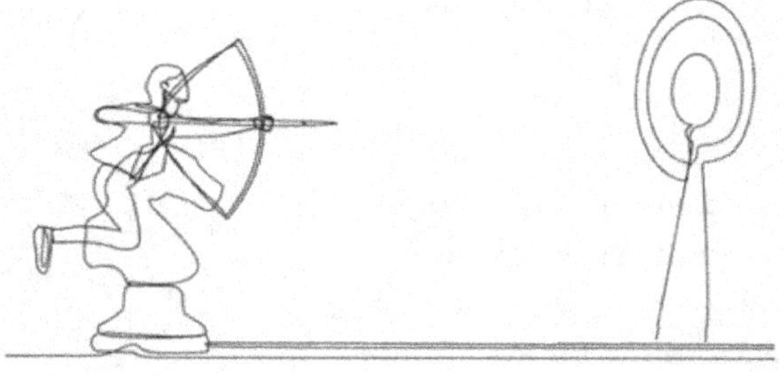

Find your *why*,
Explore *what* your heart beats for.
Focus on the *how*,
Believe in *who* you want to be.
The universe will pave the way,
To *where* and *when* reality transforms
You will see.
Defying all limitations,
Like a phoenix, you rise,
As long as constellations exist,
You'll shine and arise.

When the world tries to cage you,
Just spread your wings wide,
Being the architect of your life,
Let your dreams be your guide.

In the tapestry of life,
Your thread is unique,
Weaving tales of strength,
Giving voice to the meek.

Congratulate yourself...
When they laugh and doubt,
Set your venture.
You, the solitary seer,
Seek the path less traveled
That lights the future.
Be the unique unicorn
In the field of horses...

One day, they'll celebrate you,
Sing your tale,
Saying, "Yes, we knew—
You were always a spark, destined to prevail...!"

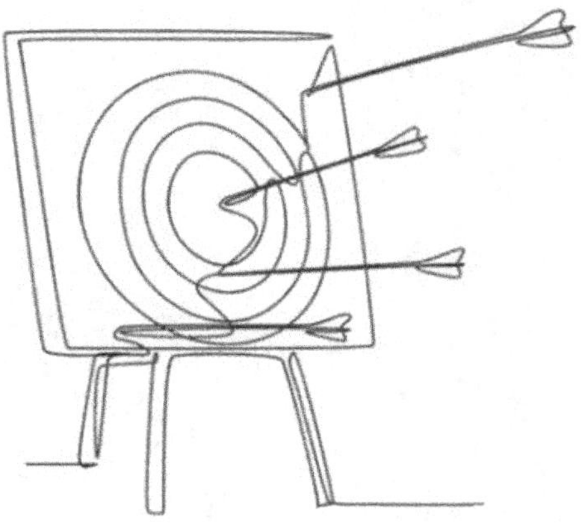

12. Chronicles of Canopy

Standing alone through endless ages,
My ancient roots embrace Mother Earth's stages.
If you can steal a moment from life's swift pace,
Ask me—I hold a thousand tales to tell,
Of innocence and fleeting joys
Beneath an azure spell.

Evoking nostalgia, moments flash—
Children swinging, playing hide and seek,
Golden sun rays dancing
Through my giant canopy,
Villagers gathered in the evening square,
Spinning tales of wonder, lessons, and care.

A gust of wind, the rustling leaves,
Sparrows twitter, squirrels weave.
A home for birds, their rhythmic dances,
A sanctuary of life, rich in glances.

Golden sunlight glistened on my leaves,
Lullabies hummed as the night wove dreams.
From fairy tales to whispered prayers,
Beneath my shadow, I have seen—
A child's laughter, a father's hope,
A mother's happy tears.
Small festivals with simple delight,
People rejoicing in the soft moonlight.
Innocence and simplicity at their best,
I stood as witness—grateful and blessed.

Oh, alas! Gone are those days,
Swept away by the ceaseless race.

No one pauses to stand and stare;
My shade lies empty; no soul finds care.
Children no longer play beneath my boughs,
Their giggles lost in digital vows.
Eyes glued to screens miss open skies,
Their heads bowed, their spirits tied.
Everywhere, filters abound;
People chase material pursuits.

Vehicles scream on endless roads,
Smoke clouds the air where life once flowed.
My companions, the trees, have all fallen down,
Replaced by towers that shadow the town.
Concrete confines bind Mother Earth,
Silencing songs of joy and mirth.

My branches weep beneath layers of dust,
Choked by winds I no longer trust.
Blurring machine hums fill the air,
As birds sing dirges for dreams once fair.
The soil beneath me cracks and sighs,
Thirsting for rain, for open skies.

Oh humanity!
Chasing a thirst, a distant mirage—
Look within—you're trapped in a virtual cage.
Can you hear my suffocating scream?
Will you lift your eyes and truly see?

While you seek another planet to live,
You forget what Mother Earth is eager to give.
Benevolent, nurturing, and divine,
She waits—ready to heal in time.
No need for distant galaxies to roam;
Our Earth is enough, a wondrous home.

Return to the Earth, to what you've lost,
Don't let "reduce, reuse, recycle"
Remain just a slogan.
The time has come to give back to Mother Earth,
For what she has always given to you.

She doesn't need your money or material gain—
Only your tender touch, your care.
Or else, be ready for extinction's bitter fare.

With quiet hope,
I hold the chronicles of my canopy, waiting—
For souls to reawaken,
For the seasons to turn,
For life to rise, like tides, from pensive pain.

Oh Supreme!
Will there be any soul left to hear,
When the world I earnestly long for reappears?

13. Untouched

In the rush of traffic, fast and wild,
Breathing air so choked,
Beneath the scorching sun,
With a thousand complaints,
I stood there, brewing frustration.

Amidst the traffic blurs and frantic pace,
My gaze shifted to the slums nearby.
There, I saw a frail girl, unscathed by noise,
Hands clasped gently,
Eyes closed tight, lost in prayer's poise.

Her crutches lay aside, with a prosthetic leg,
Her parched lips moved slow,
As if each word was a fragile prayer.
Brown tangled curls framed her delicate face,
A sublime serenity in a chaotic place.

In a world of disarray, with a heart at peace,
Her quiet prayer made my turmoil cease.
"What are you doing?" I asked, surprised.
"Thanking God," she said,
Her voice soft, yet charged with light.

No anger, no complaint, no grief to share,
Just heartfelt gratitude floating in the air.
The sun's harsh rays, once cruel, now warm—
A blessing wrapped in the morning's charm.

I wondered how she found peace in the storm,
With the world around her twisted and worn.
While I wrestled with burdens, lost in my strife,
She stood tall, defying limits, embracing life.

Like a warrior, carrying resilience's crusade,
She rose, unshaken, in courage arrayed.
"Where are you going?" I asked once more.
"To school," she replied, dreams set to soar.

"I am enough; I am unstoppable."
Her radiant face revealed a truth pure,
"I don't have this," or "It didn't go my way—"
We fill our lives with complaints each day.

While my vision clouded,
Heart heavy with dismay,
Counting life's flaws, laden with despair,
She, with sparkling eyes and dreams in sight,
Moved through life, with no pause, no fright.

And in that stillness, her gratitude burned bright,
A harbinger of hope, a beacon of light.
While I stood there, my heart took flight.
She walked on, free, showing me the way,
To find peace in the moment, to cherish today.

Chasing perfection, we grumble as time slips by,
Feeling life's weight too immense,
Each small burden, we magnify.
Why not magnify the joy life gives instead?
Let complaints evaporate; let beauty persist.

Humming through discord,
Life becomes a beautiful song.
With gratitude, we embrace
The moments that come along.

As we witness every new dawn,
Let's offer gratitude to The Divine,
For the gift of life,
For the source of light,
In every breath, let's count the blessings,
A grateful heart unfolds endless miracles.

Like a child chasing
butterflies,
Each day, we chase
fleeting happiness.

Let's pause and think;
Instead of chasing, can we create?
Instead of complaining, can we compliment?

As a garden's beauty draws
Butterflies with grace,
A peaceful mind, steeped in gratitude,
Heralds happiness to embrace.

14. Beyond Cosmic Maze

Let's go,
Beyond the azure sky,
Where dreams take flight,
Search for a ravishing globe
Bathed in celestial light.
Amid the galaxies,
Unraveling the mysteries untold,
Where stars whisper secrets,
And the cosmos unfolds.

Where, as a herald of hope and hilarity,
The sun rises on the horizon,
Painting hues of clarity.
Its golden rays expel the dark clouds of dismay,
Illuminating paths where shadows cannot stay.

The gleaming fountain,
With its sweet, eternal murmur,
Dances in delight,
A hymn of life in constant fervor.
It breaks the monotony of somber hearts,
Weaving melodies where despair departs.

Elegant flowers bloom with enchanting aroma,
Their petals unfurl,
A symphony of vibrant persona.
Together, they inaugurate
An era of joy and jubilation,
A celebration of life,
A world's transformation.

May there be no monarchy of macabre hearts,
No reign of shadows
Tearing fragile dreams apart.
Let love and harmony reign
As a seraphic drizzle,
Washing away hatred,
Soothing the world's puzzle.

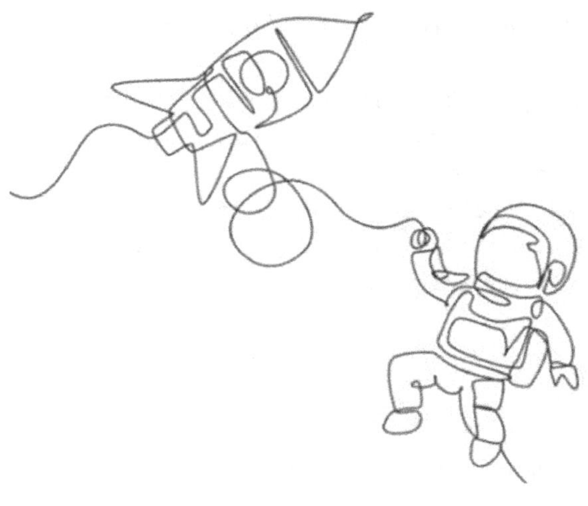

Let every soul shed
The garbage of noxious despair,
And rise anew, lighter, freer, without a care.
For when the gloomy globe begins to glisten,
Every heart will find its rhythm,
Every voice will listen.

Let's wander where the galaxies hold their choir,
Where stars ignite dreams, setting hearts on fire.
Let's lose ourselves in the infinite expanse above,
A realm of wonder, beauty, and undying love.

Oh, let's go—
Beyond the azure sky, beyond our limited gaze,
To a world of marvels, through the cosmic maze.
Let's dare to dream, to heal, to rebuild anew,
A planet of peace, of harmony, for me and you.

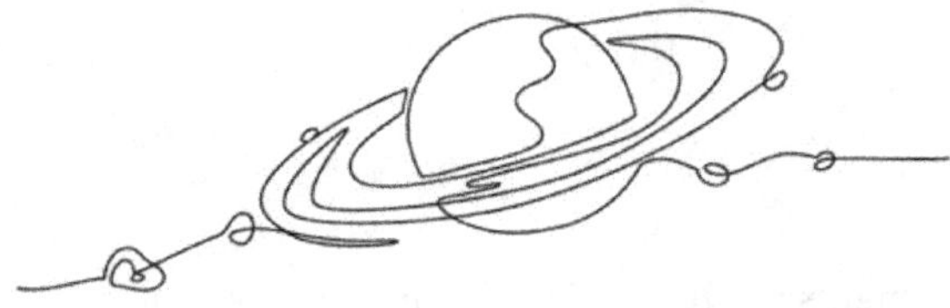

15. Through the Pixels

Traversing through augmented reality,
With keystrokes and scrolls,
Clicks and blinks,
I drift and immerse in the digital ocean.
Beneath virtual waves, I dive deep,
Thoughts buoyed in Bernoulli's sweep.
In endless blue, nostalgia whispers,
A warm breeze where
Moments dance and glisten.

Moments flash; I travel down memory lane,
Meeting the carefree girl
With an innocent giggle again.
Her joy, like little things, shines bright,
Spreading harmony's spectrum,
Her eyes twinkle with delight.

Standing on life's zigzag roads,
I find her there,
Jumping through hopscotch squares
Without a care.
Bobbing and weaving in the wind
Like a fragile kite,
Chasing dreams, her spirit soars, taking flight.

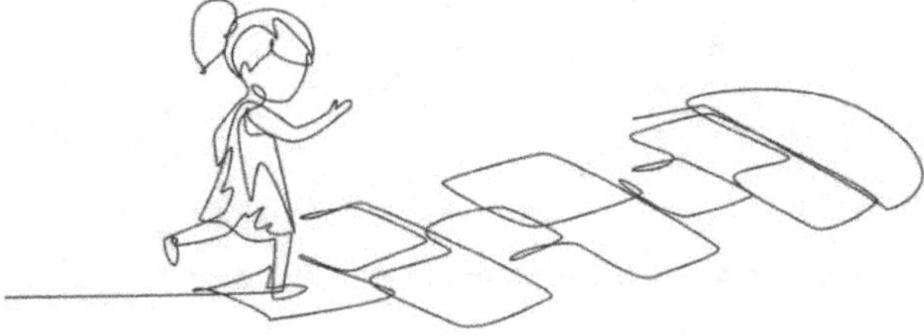

Like a swaying dandelion
On a breezy afternoon,
Spinning happiness,
She plays hide-and-seek in a tiny cocoon.
Sailing paper boats in a gentle drizzle,
I find her splashing through the muddy puddle.

In silvery moonlight, sometimes I see her,
Counting blinking stars,
Wrapped in warmth, a gentle cuddle.
With pencils and crayons,
She colors her magical world,
In jubilant hues, her ambitions unfurl.

Sometimes she visits Alice in her Wonderland,
Other times, I find her in Hogwarts' grand land,
Jumping through trees in Mowgli's jungle,
With Baloo and Bagheera,
She tumbles and jumbles.
Again, I see her scared by Maleficent's curse,

As Princess Aurora awakens in her universe.
With a honey pot,
Winnie the Pooh welcomes her
To the Hundred Acre Wood,
And sometimes...
She lands in the tiny cottage
With Red Riding Hood.

Golden moments disperse through life's prism,
Creating a rainbow in a ravishing rhythm.
From nostalgic whirls
To the clock's pendulum sound,
I wake to infinite chaos
Where restless races abound.
Amid life's countless twists and turns,
I embrace life's paradox
With Schrödinger's smile,
Diving into a divine ocean...!!!

16. The Treasure Chest

On a breezy afternoon,
Submerge in gentle swirls
From a mug of coffee.
Pause the clock,
Savor the present in the whirl of thoughts!

Watch a child's innocent giggles,
Sparkling eyes while chasing bubbles,
Listen to the sound of waves,
Build sandcastles ashore,
Walk on the beach,
Collect the seashells,
Witness the crimson sun
Gliding down the far horizon.

Watch a sunrise in the azure sky,
Soaring above clouds, little birdies fly.
Sunrays dance through fluffy clouds,
A blade of grass glimmers with morning dew!

Cool breeze on a summer afternoon,
Pitter-patter of rain, a gentle tune.
Falling leaves in autumn, colors bright,
Flowers bloom on spring days, pure delight.

Plant a sapling with tender care,
Feed the animals with a gentle share.
A kind act to bring a smile so bright,
A soulful prayer to the divine's light.

Thrilling the heart and soothing the soul,
Read an old book, travel down memory's lane.
Inhale the aroma of books
In the vintage library,
Venturing forth on an expedition,
Treasures to unveil.

A talk with a good friend,
A walk in beautiful weather,
A tender hug from Mother,
A gentle pat from Father,
In the old album, lovely moments glitter.

On a rainy evening,
Sip a cup of tea by a blurry windowpane,
In the chaos of life,
Steal away some still moments.
Listen to an old melody while silence prevails,

These quiet moments
Grant us space to reflect,
Leaving behind the hustle and bustle,
Let's rejuvenate.
As twilight whispers,
Shadows softly blend,
Each memory a gem,
A story without end.
Embrace the fleeting moments,
Let laughter unfold,
For in these simple joys,
Our hearts are truly bold.

Let us gather these moments,
Woven with care,
Like small pearls strung in an elegant garland.
Simple joys fill our days with happiness,
Making life jubilant and grand...!

17. The Conquest

"Oh... Mother!
You said... I am born free.
Singing my happiest song
I dared to touch
Where the Earth meets the sky
I opened my wings and flapped
With all my power
My joy evaporated soon,
And I dashed miserably to that tall tower...

Momma! I am tired of
The plethora of perilous trials...
Please convey to me why I should fly.
How cruel of you to send me
Alone to the gigantic sky!
Don't you pity my tiny little wings...
Tired... faded with the sun's scorching heat...!

Let me enjoy my life with my tiny jumps...!
The outer world is so malignant...
Don't you know devils are everywhere...
Let me relish and sleep in my cozy nest...!

What if the blazing sun burns
My fragile plumage...?
What if I end up as a delicious
Snack of that cruel hunter...?

Why do you force me to fly...?
I kept your words... I soared to the sky...
Don't you know I landed up
In that cactus field and tore my wings!
Still, you want me to learn to fly?"
The dejected little eaglet uttered to the mother.

"Oh Baby...!
You are born to fly...
You are born to own the vast azure sky
Not to crawl and jump...
Almighty has gifted you the wings...
Soar high beyond the clouds
Whatever darkness if any storm brings...!

Oh, my dear child...! Just look around...
When the whole world is your home...
Why do you want to
Restrict it to a little dome?
With vivid colors,
Our planet is magnanimously beautiful
During the journey of life,
Traveling gets you many
Friends wonderful...

Go and chase the blazing Sun
With your burning desire
Don't be afraid of the failures, my little one...
Ignite the dejection on the pyre!

Failures teach you... guide you...
Shape you more than success...
Just believe in yourself...
Learning from every failure,
Rise with confidence.

Breaking the chains of fear,
Liberate thyself from mind prison
Fly... Fly and Fly my little one...
Behold! Get spellbound with
Mother Nature's spectacular vision...!"
The mother Eagle explained to her little one.

The little eaglet looks up to the golden sky
The tranquility mesmerizes her
The amalgamation of hope
And hilarity propels her to fly
Oh, how superbly the serene vista eradicates
The ignorance of her mind sky...!
The cool breeze propels her...
With all answers,
The little birdie soars with joy...
Finding her way beyond the azure horizon...
In no time, she rises above the clouds...
Conquering the crimson sky...!!!

18. Seraphic Symphony

Beyond the physical realm,
Where sensorium cease,
In a boundless peace,
You expand to infinity...!

Sometimes as a gust of wind,
You refresh the soul,
Passing through rustling leaves,
You spread tranquility.
Sometimes on the far horizon,
Like the orange sun
As the herald of eternal light,
You rise...
Sometimes on the velvet night,
As the gibbous moon
Among distant pearly stars,
You shine bright.

Beyond countless Andromedas,
Swirling in cosmic mist,
As neutrinos, You are a phantom,
Mingling with dust adrift.

In the endless blue of ancient oceans,
Like a sacred pulse, You flow,
As morning dew on blades of grass,
You reflect with a diamond glow.

In majestic mountains, arching rainbows
Paint the sky sublime,
In lush green valleys, You dwell in rivers' ripples
Blending Earth and divine.

The petite pebbles and tall trees
Bear great tenacity,
Of that fragile flower,
The delicate petals depict Your seraphic artistry.
Like the sunbeam gleaming on icicles bright,
You appear in a child's giggles, pure delight.

As the waterfall's endless waves
Cascade in ethereal embrace,
You shine in a mother's swaddle
With tender, caring grace.

Still, some scream in despair,
"You do not exist,"
Oh Omnipresent, transcending all
Peripheries, everywhere, You persist...!!!

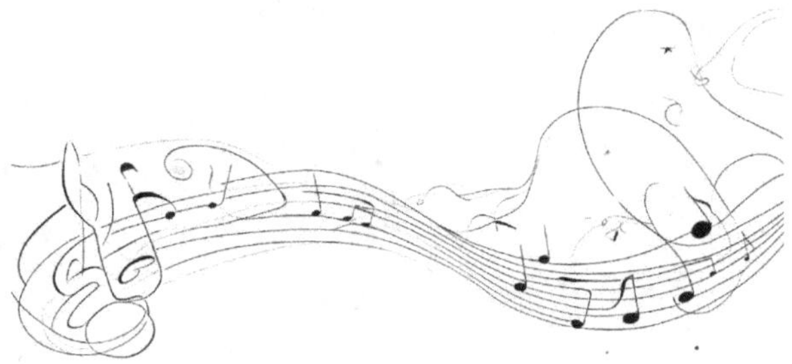

19. The Atlas

Defying the scorching sun's fierce glare,
Drenching in the ceaseless rain,
Denying the warmth on biting winter nights,
You build a world
Where my dreams could flourish.

Shielding me from edges cruel and sharp,
Leading me through shadows in the darkest night.
Like the North Star, your wisdom shines,
You are my beacon, my guiding light.

Like a warrior,
You silently nurture my hopes,
Metamorphosing them into reality.
You guard the castle of my dreams,
Fighting fiercely against
Superstitious dogmas
And illiterate stigmas.

Woven from the threads of patience,
Your armor is stitched with sacrifice,
Polished by the tears you never let fall.
Fighting silent battles with indomitable will,
You build a fortress around me,
A safe haven for my unwavering dreams,
Untouched by the harsh world's wind.

Each mocking word
That wounds my brittle heart,
I know it pierces you deeper,
Yet you never part.
Your silent strength,
A shield so vast,
Guarding my life's voyage
From storms that pass.

I have seen you, sometimes,
When exhaustion defeats you;
Stressed by the weight of pain,
Yet, like the Atlas,
You carry the globe
Of responsibilities alone,
Holding my fragile dreams,
Always protecting them
From shattering into pieces.

Never can I forget, those darkest hours,
Wrestling with the chasm of despair,
When I have seen shadows creep,
Even then your strength whispers hope,
Teaching me how to dream and cope.

You rise like a Phoenix, from ashes reborn,
Shattering the chains of dismay.
You teach me to soar the endless sky,
To conquer the battles, and always try.

Not just academics in the temple of education,
As a nation builder,
You teach life's deeper foundation.
Thousands of students bear the testament,
To lessons profound, your noble intent.

The ABCs of life, you gently unfold,
A guide through storms, steadfast and bold.
You are the propeller of my life's canoe,
A compass pointing to paths anew.

Through currents fierce and waters wide,
You steer my soul with wisdom as the tide.
A bonfire of light, unwavering, true,
Shaping dreams with a visionary hue.

As a splendid author, you ignite the little souls,
With compassion
And thousands of life lessons untold.
I pray to the Almighty,
May you pen stories forever,
Contributing to the world,
Though it's distracted by virtual pleasures.

The world is busy chasing fleeting happiness,
Ignoring the literary gifts,
The heart's true richness.
My love for literature is inherited from you,
You nurture the poetess; in me it grew.

I hope one day I can carry
Your legacy with pride,
May my pen contribute to society, far and wide.
In the echoes of your words, I find my way,
To write, to inspire, and to brighten each day.

I may go unseen in the world of others,
A shadow fading in their fleeting wonders.
But in your tiny kingdom, I always reign,
A throne of warmth where stars align.

The world may rush by, distant and cold,
Yet here, I am treasured, more than gold.
Your love crowns me with a glow divine,
A princess cherished forever
In your sacred realm.

Oh, my great nurturer, my beloved father!
Thank you from the core of my heart,
For everything you've done
Since the day I was born,
It is because of you that
I stand in this world, reborn.

For your vision, your love,
Your unwavering care,
I strive to embody the values
You've instilled, so rare.
May I become the someone
You've dreamed of, one day,
Living your hopes in each word I say.

With every step, I carry your dream,
Guided by your wisdom, like a steady beam.
I must have done virtues
To be born as your daughter,
In your sublime legacy,
I find strength, unaltered,
Immensely grateful to you,
Now and forever,
A love that will endure,
No matter the weather.

I pray to the Divine Power
For your healthy, long life,
May you continue to inspire a thousand souls,
Through your words, your wisdom, your strife,
Guiding hearts, making broken spirits whole!

May your light shine bright,
Endless now and always,
A flame that guides through all of life's maze!!!

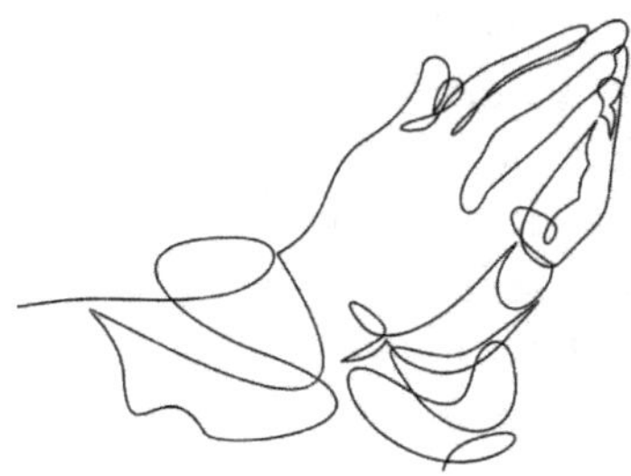

20. The Gravity

In the quiet of the night,
I have seen her—
Kneeling, hands folded, eyes closed,
Whispering prayers to the Almighty,
For my well-being,
For my wounds to heal,
For my present to thrive,
And for my future to flourish,
Against life's unseen tornados.
As a silent shield, her prayers safeguard me.

As I grow and drift farther away,
From her tiny nest,
To explore the vast world,
Away from the warmth of her plumage,
I feel her more in this oblivious world
Where no one has time to stand and stare.
How solitary I am,
While everyone races for happiness,
Like a mirage.

But when I see her,
I feel her strength
Chasing time and distance,
Racing against locomotives,
Just for a fleeting glimpse of me.
Knowing it will vanish in seconds,
Yet, for her, those moments
Are worth more than eternity.
In those few heartbeats,
I see her unwavering love
A love that pulls like centripetal force,
Defying time and space,
Pulling me back
To her affectionate cove.

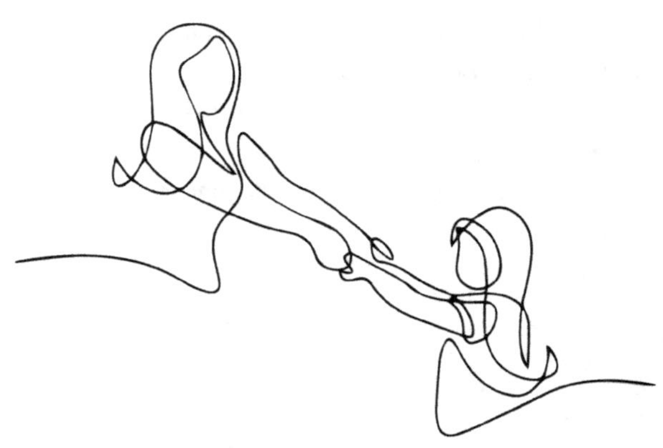

Like restless waves in a vast, unruly sea,
Life offers its share of challenges.
But with her love beside me,
I stand resolute, unshaken.
Amidst the swirling waves,
I embark on an expedition,
A hot air balloon soaring high.

Her guidance, a lighthouse in the dark,
Illuminates my path,
Instilling belief in my boundless potential.
Her presence, serene and sublime,
A beacon of hope,
A tender reminder
That with her by my side,
I can conquer it all.
Defying distance,

She is the angel sent by the Almighty.
With her magic wand,
She fulfills my every wish without saying a word.
With tender care,
She crafts invisible wings,
Empowering me to soar,
To reach for the azure horizon beyond my sight.

She nurtures me with boundless love,
Like the Sun cradles a growing plant,
Pouring warmth and light into every leaf.
As the constant, guiding force,
She is the Sun of my life.
Like gravity,
She pulls all joys that cling to my heart,
Binding them with her quiet strength,
Her endless devotion.

In her arms, I find courage.
In her eyes, I see dreams fulfilled.
With her by my side,
I am hopeful—
The zenith of success within my reach.
Even in her absence,
Her love remains,
A soft echo in the chambers of my heart.
Like the Northern Star, she is my compass,
Guiding my path when I am lost,
Ensuring my way is bright,
Even when shadows loom.

Her thoughts,
Like centrifugal force,
Push me forward,
Defeating the odds,
Marching ahead on life's journey,
Keeping me twined to the depths of her heart.

Thank you, dear Mother,
From the core of my heart,
For every sacrifice,
Every silent prayer,
Every quiet act of love.
I am who I am,
Because of you.
And with every step,
I carry your strength,
Your spirit,
Your endless grace—
The shape of you.

Oh Almighty,
How blessed am I,
Beyond measure,
To walk life's journey
With her unwavering presence.
I pray for her health and well-being,
May she be hale and hearty, always.
With Your Divine presence…!
May she remain the eternal light in my life,
Now and always…!!!

21. Towards Tranquility

Oh Supreme Soul...!
In the endless blue,
With peace and harmony,
Like a voyage heads to a sublime harbor,
Washing away the agonies,
The oscillations within my heart
Find tranquility
In Your celestial armor.

In the silence of twilight dawn,
My pensive heart submerged,
In an ocean of countless thoughts!
Leaving behind the blurred hums of life,
I venture forth, unburdened,
Into the azure sea's boundless embrace!

The sun rests gently in the horizon's lap,
While waves caress the shore,
Whispering secrets, ancient and profound,
Each crest cradling a tale untold.

The horizon stretches infinitely,
A union of Earth and Divine.
As a harbinger of hope, the sun ascends,
Golden rays dance on rippling waters,
Hues of serenity intertwine.

No chaotic voices, no distant cries,
Only the rhythms of the tides—
A soothing solace for the seeking soul.
Confusion dissolves,
And I feel the pulse of the Divine inside.

In blissful solitude, I stand,
Wrapped in a tender veil of peace.
This sacred stillness reminds me
That I belong
That I am part of an endless, melodious song.

In this quiet communion,
I feel You stir within my heart.
Oh, Almighty...
You are the Omnipresent,
Beyond the bounds of time and space.
You are here—in the waves, in the breeze,
In every moment, every place.

I am sorry for the complaints I voiced,
For seeing lack amidst life's flow,
For questioning Your perfect design,
And missing the blessings I did not know.

Please forgive me for moments of doubt,
When storms within shut Your light out.
When I stumbled, lost in despair,
Not feeling Your seraphic grace was there.

Thank You for holding my hands,
Through both joy and pain,
For lifting me when I could not stand,
For protecting me through the sun and rain.

For love unspoken, yet always near,
For whispers of hope I failed to hear.
I love You—in awe of infinity's grace,
In Your vast embrace, I find my place.

In the crests and troughs of life,
Let me offer my gratitude...
With Your greatest benevolence,
You always steer me to high amplitude.

As the dawn breaks through the night,
I stand, mesmerized by tender golden light,
Knowing I have found my way,
In Your Divine embrace, at the break of day...!!!

9 789367 396469